D0463062

HISTORY OF FUN STUFF

The Stellar Story of Space Travel

by Patricia Lakin
illustrated by Scott Burroughs

Ready-to-Read

Simon Spotlight
New York   London   Toronto   Sydney   New Delhi

SIMON SPOTLIGHT
An imprint of Simon & Schuster Children's Publishing Division
1230 Avenue of the Americas, New York, New York 10020
This Simon Spotlight edition February 2016
Text copyright © 2016 by Simon & Schuster, Inc.
Illustrations copyright © 2016 by Scott Burroughs
For information about special discounts for bulk purchases, please contact Simon & Schuster Special Sales at
1-866-506-1949 or business@simonandschuster.com.
Manufactured in the United States of America 1215 LAK
2 4 6 8 10 9 7 5 3 1
Library of Congress Cataloging-in-Publication Data
Lakin, Patricia, 1944- author.
The stellar story of space travel / by Patricia Lakin ; illustrated by Scott Burroughs.
pages cm. — (Ready-to-read) (History of fun stuff)
Audience: Ages 6-8
1. Space flight—Juvenile literature. 2. Astronautics—History—Juvenile literature. 3. Space race—History—
Juvenile literature. 4. Outer space—Exploration—Juvenile literature. I. Burroughs, Scott, illustrator. II. Title.
III. Series: History of fun stuff. IV. Series: Ready-to-read. Level three, Megastar reader!
TL793.L235 2016
629.4'1—dc23
2015033675
ISBN 978-1-4814-5624-1 (hc)
ISBN 978-1-4814-5623-4 (pbk)
ISBN 978-1-4814-5625-8 (eBook)

CONTENTS

CHAPTER 1
The First Astronomers

Twinkle, twinkle, little star,
How I wonder what you are!

If you ever looked up at the sky and wondered, then welcome to the club. You are like millions before you. In ancient times people had no experts to ask, equipment to use, or science books to read. They looked, studied, and made guesses about outer space. Some guesses were correct, some not.

Today with a simple telescope you can see stars clearly. You might have heard that people have traveled into space *and* landed on the Moon. But do you know who the first space explorers were? And what discoveries they made? Or what science-fiction book predicted the future?

By the time you finish reading this book, you'll know the answers to all those questions and more. You will be a History of Fun Stuff Expert on space travel!

Ancient people who studied the sky were the first astronomers. Astronomy [uh-STRON-uh-mee] is the science of studying outer space. Early astronomers realized that many stars stayed in a set pattern even as they moved across the sky.

They called those patterns constellations [kon-stuh-LAY-shuns]. Early sailors and land travelers looked up at the sky and used the positions of the constellations to guide them on their way.

Ancient astronomers observed other objects in the sky that moved, like the Sun and the Moon. Huge structures were built. The shadows the buildings made on the ground or the position of the objects in the sky in relation to the structures told everyone the time and season. These buildings were the first clocks and calendars.

Stonehenge (Ancient England)

Kukulkan Pyramid (Ancient Mexico)

Temple of Amun-Ra at Karnak (Ancient Egypt)

Early astronomers also noticed some objects in the sky that were different from stars, but smaller than the Sun and Moon. They called them planets. They noted that the planets moved in a circlelike path around our home planet, Earth. The famous Greek thinker Aristotle proved that Earth was shaped like a ball or sphere around 350 BC. But he believed everything circled around Earth.

More than a thousand years later the Polish astronomer Nicolaus Copernicus came to believe that the planets circled around the Sun. He knew his discovery would make people furious and scared, having their long-held beliefs questioned. He only shared some of his ideas just before he died in 1543.

The Italian Galileo Galilei was the first astronomer to take the newly invented spyglass that magnified objects and turn it into a telescope. His studies led him to agree with Copernicus. In 1632 he spoke out and was punished for his beliefs. Galileo was kept a prisoner in his home until his death in 1642.

English physicist Isaac Newton was born the year Galileo died. In 1687 Newton published his discovery—a force on Earth called gravity. It's what keeps objects on Earth from floating into space. And it's gravity that keeps planets on their path. That path, Newton discovered, is oval shaped, not round. Newton's work also proved that Copernicus and Galileo had been right—the Sun is the center of our solar system. In other words, the Earth and the other planets in our solar system orbit around the Sun.

CHAPTER 2
The Space Race Begins!

As time passed, astronomers wanted to get closer to these stars and planets. For hundreds of years people had been working on something that would eventually lead to a way to travel into space—the rocket! Around the year 1000 the Chinese created fireworks, which are really tiny rockets. Later they used them when they fought their battles by strapping fireworks onto their arrows. The lit rocket shot forward and carried the attached arrow farther and faster than ever.

After Isaac Newton's discovery, scientists knew that rockets had to fight against gravity in order to lift off the ground. The more fuel used, the farther the rocket could go.

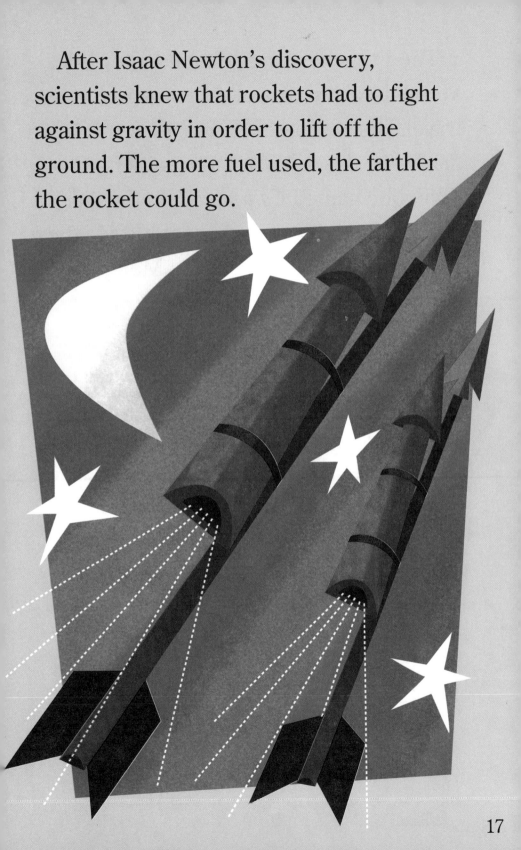

The French science-fiction writer Jules Verne dreamed of rockets and space travel. His 1865 book, *From the Earth to the Moon,* described a three-passenger rocket he named *Columbiad.* In the story the rocket was launched from Florida, flew into space, and landed on the Moon.

Actual scientists worked to make
Verne's dream come true. In the early
twentieth century Russian scientist
Konstantin Tsiolkovsky came up with the
idea of using liquid fuel to power rockets.
Unlike powder, which fuels fireworks,
liquid fuel can last a long time. It's still
used to fuel rockets today. American
scientist Robert Goddard also used liquid
fuel. In 1926 his rocket made history by
being the first to lift off.

On October 4, 1957, the Soviet Union, a confederation of European and Asian countries including Russia and Ukraine, launched a rocket. The rocket carried *Sputnik*, the first man-made satellite, into space. In November their second satellite was launched. This one carried a dog named Laika.

The United States was amazed at what the Soviet Union had done. The US was also working on developing rockets, but *Sputnik*'s success put the Soviet Union way ahead. *Sputnik* sparked the start of the Space Race between the Soviet Union and the United States. Ever since the end of World War II each of these powerful nations had been suspicious of the other. Who had the strongest army? Who had more advanced technology?

Soon after *Sputnik* the US president, Dwight D. Eisenhower, signed a bill that created the National Aeronautics and Space Agency, or NASA. NASA's mission: Explore outer space.

CHAPTER 3
3-2-1 Blast Off!: The Space Race Continues

January 31, 1958, was a win for the US in the Space Race. They successfully launched the satellite *Explorer 1*. But the Soviet scientists weren't resting. In April 1961 they sent the first man into space. Yuri Gagarin orbited once around Earth. The Soviet Union called their space explorers cosmonauts. The US used the term astronaut. On May 5, 1961, astronaut Alan Shepard became the first American to travel into space. Unlike Gagarin, who left his spacecraft when returning to Earth and landed by parachute, Shepard landed safely inside his space capsule.

Also unlike the Soviet mission, everything about the American mission was televised. People all over the world watched as Alan Shepard went up into space and came back.

For the next few years the United States and the Soviet Union tried to outdo the other. By 1965 Russia seemed to be in the lead when cosmonaut Alexei Leonov left his capsule and floated in space for ten minutes.

But then, that same year, US Astronaut Edward White II floated in space for twenty-three minutes! Those were great accomplishments, but landing on the moon was the big goal for both countries.

In 1969 the US accomplished
something that Jules Verne had written
about 104 years earlier. On July 16 the
US launched a rocket from Florida. It
carried three astronauts, Michael Collins,
Neil Armstrong, and Buzz Aldrin. Their
command module was named *Columbia*,
after Verne's capsule, *Columbiad*. Four
days later, Armstrong and then Aldrin
left the command module, landed on the
moon, and planted the American flag on
its surface. It was a monumental victory.

These Americans were the first humans on the moon. But scientists knew the moon held more secrets. In 1971 and 1972 the US successfully sent up three lunar vehicles, or rovers, with astronauts to operate them. The team landed on the moon, collected rocks, and brought them back for scientists to study.

By now relations between the Soviet Union and the US had improved. In July 1975 a US and a Soviet spacecraft orbited in space at the same time. As planned, the American astronaut and the Soviet cosmonaut met in space and shook hands. The Space Race was officially over.

But space exploration was still expanding.

In 1977 Sally Ride applied to be a NASA astronaut, and she went on to become the first American woman in space. That same year the space probes *Voyager 1* and *Voyager 2* were sent into space. Their mission: Travel to the farthest planets in our solar system to gather and send back information and pictures. The *Voyager*s were built to last for five years.

Sadly, not all of NASA's missions in space were successful. On a cold Florida morning in January 1986 the spacecraft *Challenger* launched. It carried a crew of seven. A little more than a minute after liftoff the rocket carrying *Challenger* exploded. All aboard were killed. Later, scientists discovered that a sealing ring in the fuel tank had broken, which may have caused the explosion. The world was saddened.

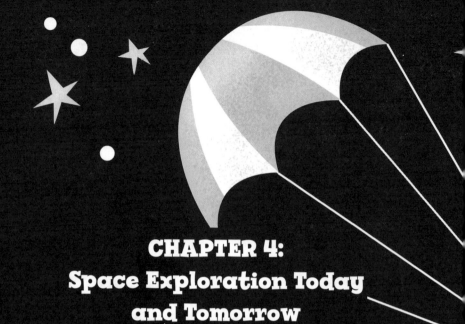

CHAPTER 4:
Space Exploration Today and Tomorrow

Space exploration had to go on. Sending people into space wasn't the only way to do it. And some planets are so far away that no person could make the trip—at least not currently. Mars is the closest planet to Earth and is about 140 million miles away! Mechanical robots, used during the Space Race, were the answer. But scientists didn't want the robots to crash or get damaged upon landing. In the late 1990s they came up with a clever solution for the *Mars Pathfinder*. Once it reached

Mars, parachutes opened and lowered it down. Then airbags popped up so that it bounced safely on the surface of Mars. *Mars Pathfinder* analyzed samples of rock and dirt and transmitted its findings back to Earth for scientists to study.

Since the 1960s, the US and other countries have sent unmanned satellites up to orbit the Earth. Some are weather satellites. They send back images of Earth that show clear skies, patches of clouds, or storms that are forming. That information helps us prepare for upcoming weather. Communication satellites either receive signals from Earth or bounce them back to Earth. They're used when we make some phone calls or tune in to some radio stations or watch some television channels.

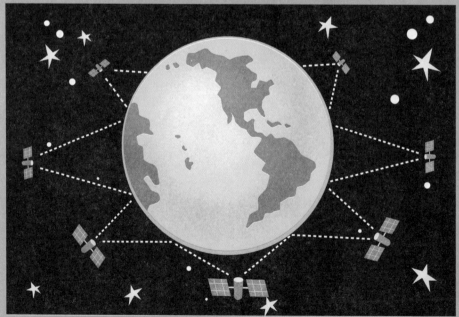

Scientists also rely on other unmanned satellites called space probes. *Voyager 1* and *Voyager 2* are the space probes that were only supposed to last until 1982. They are *still* hurtling far off into space. In 2012 *Voyager 1* entered the space beyond the planets in our solar system, called interstellar space. *Voyager 1* has now traveled farther than anyone or anything from Earth has ever traveled before.

Today scientists from all over the world realize that information we gather from outer space needs to be shared. In the late 1990s many countries worked together to launch the International Space Station, or ISS.

Since 2000, men and women from a variety of countries have taken turns living on board the ISS. It is a huge orbiting beehive of scientific activity. Astronauts, scientists, and other experts conduct experiments there. It gives them the

chance to do research with no pull of gravity.

One of the things these experts are studying is how the human body is affected in space with no gravity. Bones and muscles weaken. How can people keep their bodies strong? This research will lead to solutions for people who will travel and one day may live in space.

Today you don't have to be an astronaut to go into orbit. In the early 2000s a few millionaires who passed a physical test went aboard the International Space Station. One person paid $35 million for his ticket. Another got a bargain and paid $20 million! More and more, scientists in many countries realize that space travel

needs to be open to other citizens. One businessperson has created a spacecraft and is selling tickets for $250,000 each. The hope is that traveling into outer space will become cheaper and more common. Who knows? If you are in shape, in a few years you may be planning your vacation—in outer space.

SPACE RESORT

HISTORY
OF FUN STUFF
EXPERT
ON
SPACE
TRAVEL

Congratulations! You've come to the end of this book. You're now an official History of Fun Stuff Expert on space travel. Go ahead and impress your friends and family with all the cool things you know about space. And the next time you gaze up at the sky, remember everything you've learned and ask yourself: Do you want to go up to space someday?

Hey, kids! Now that you're an expert on the history of space travel, turn the page to learn even more about space travel and some astronomy, world cultures, and literature along the way!

Day and Night

You probably know that the Earth orbits around the Sun, and that it takes the Earth one year to complete one full orbit. But did you know that the Earth spins as it orbits?

Just like a ballet dancer spins on his or her toes, the Earth spins on its axis. The Earth's axis is an imaginary line that runs through the planet from the North Pole to the South Pole. The Earth rotates around this imaginary line.

You see, even though the Sun appears to travel across the sky, rising in the east in the morning and setting in the west at night, the Sun isn't actually moving at all—we are!

It takes the Earth twenty-four hours to complete one full spin on its axis. At any given moment it's daytime for the half of the Earth that is being lit by the Sun. But at the same time the side of the Earth that is facing away from the Sun is experiencing nighttime.

If you have a globe and a flashlight at home, you can try this yourself! Shine a flashlight on the globe and have a friend spin the globe around slowly. Notice how the side facing the flashlight is always bright, while the side opposite the flashlight is always dark, just like the day and night!

The Stars that Shaped the Sky

In ancient times people looked at the stars and saw pictures. Each picture, called a constellation, had its own story. These stories were told by people all over the world!

Orion, the Hunter—There are many stories about the Orion constellation. The ancient Greeks said Orion was a great hunter who fell in love with Artemis, the goddess of the hunt. But the ancient Egyptians associated this constellation with their god of rebirth, Osiris. This constellation is very big and very bright. In North America you can find Orion easily any time from November through February.

The Big Dipper—Believe it or not, the Big Dipper actually isn't a constellation; it's an asterism! An **asterism** is a group of stars that form part of a constellation. The Big Dipper is part of the constellation Ursa Major, or the Great Bear. Many cultures have stories about the Big Dipper. In Germany and Hungary the asterism is known as a cart or wagon, and in the United Kingdom and Ireland people see it as a plow. To find the Big Dipper from the continental United States, look to the northwest sky in the summer.

Cygnus, the Swan—Some ancient Greeks saw this constellation as Zeus, the god, disguised as a swan, but other Greeks said the swan was Orpheus, a musician who transformed into a swan after his death. The ancient Chinese also had a myth about this constellation—they saw the constellation as a bridge across the heavens. Two forbidden lovers would meet once a year by crossing the starry bridge. If you live in the continental United States, you can find Cygnus by looking for the Northern Cross, an asterism within the constellation. You can find it high in the sky during late summer.

Leo, the Lion—Leo is one of the oldest documented constellations. The ancient Greeks saw Leo as the lion that the hero Hercules killed during his twelve labors, and this same constellation was also seen as a lion by the ancient Egyptians, Sumerians, Persians, and Babylonians. In North America you can find Leo during the springtime by looking for his mane, a backward question mark.

Science Fiction That Came True!

In 1865 Jules Verne wrote about astronauts landing on the moon. No one believed it would happen—but a little more than one hundred years later, it did!

Verne wrote **science fiction**. Science fiction is a genre about imaginary scientific developments.

Verne wasn't the only writer or artist to predict something. In the late 1400s Leonardo da Vinci, the Italian artist who painted the *Mona Lisa*, drew sketches of a flying machine. He hoped that one day humans could fly in machines—and he was right.

Mark Twain, the author of *The Adventures of Huckleberry Finn*, wrote about something that resembles today's Internet back in 1898. But it wasn't just the Internet—Twain predicted social media, too! He wrote that one day we'd be able to make our thoughts public with the click of a button. Little did he know, today this system also helps space explorers communicate with people back on Earth.

In the TV show, *Star Trek: The Next Generation*, which premiered in 1987, members of the starship *Enterprise* used PADDs, or "personal access display devices." PADDs sent messages and recorded data. Now we use tablets for the same purpose.

In the late 1970s author Douglas Adams penned *The Hitchhiker's Guide to the Galaxy*. He wrote about a machine that can make any drink instantly! Today NASA is developing a 3-D food printer. The printer will make food for astronauts on long space flights. It can print a tasty pizza, made with special "ink" for the bread, sauce, and cheese.

What else are today's scientists working on? What about warp speed? Although it seems impossible now, maybe someday we will be able to launch spaceships farther into space. You can see spaceships travel at warp-speed in science-fiction movies and television shows like *Star Wars* and *Star Trek*.

What do you think life will be like in one hundred or one thousand years? Maybe we'll vacation on Saturn—or fly our very own spaceships!

Being an expert on something means you can get an awesome score on a quiz on that subject! Take this

HISTORY OF SPACE TRAVEL QUIZ

to see how much you've learned.

1. Early sailors and travelers used star patterns called what to guide them?
   a. constellations   b. black holes   c. telegrams

2. Which astronomer was the first to believe that the planets circled around the Sun?
   a. Aristotle   b. Sally Ride   c. Nicolaus Copernicus

3. What force, discovered by Newton, keeps objects on Earth from floating into space?
   a. potatoes   b. gravity   c. magnification

4. Where were rockets invented around the year 1000?
   a. China   b. the Moon   c. England

5. When did the Soviet Union launch *Sputnik*, the first man-made satellite, into space?
   a. 1957   b. 1090   c. 1832

6. Which US president signed the bill that created NASA?
   a. Teddy Roosevelt   b. James Garfield   c. Dwight D. Eisenhower

7. Unlike the first cosmonaut in space, the first American astronaut in space was able to do what?
   a. the hokey pokey   b. talk to extraterrestrials   c. land safely back on Earth inside his space capsule

8. What year did US astronauts land on the Moon for the first time?
   a. 1320   b. 1969   c. 1997

9. In the 1990s what robot did scientists send to Mars?
   a. *Mars Pathfinder*   b. *Mars Enterprise*   c. *Mars Penguin*

10. What part of space did the space probe *Voyager 1* enter in 2012?
    a. the Sun   b. groovy space   c. interstellar space

Answers: 1. a 2. c 3. b 4. a 5. a 6. c 7. c 8. b 9. a 10. c